50 Premium Restaurant Soup Dishes

By: Kelly Johnson

Table of Contents

- Lobster Bisque
- French Onion Soup
- Cream of Mushroom Soup
- Roasted Tomato Soup
- New England Clam Chowder
- Manhattan Clam Chowder
- Butternut Squash Soup
- Velouté Soup
- Chicken Velouté Soup
- French Pea Soup (Soupe au Pois)
- Seafood Chowder
- Crab Bisque
- Cream of Asparagus Soup
- Minestrone
- Potato Leek Soup
- Chicken Tortilla Soup
- Pho (Vietnamese Noodle Soup)
- Miso Soup
- Hot and Sour Soup
- Tom Yum Soup
- Thai Coconut Soup (Tom Kha)
- Beef Barley Soup
- Gazpacho
- Cream of Spinach Soup
- Lobster Corn Chowder
- Split Pea Soup
- Pumpkin Soup
- Sunchoke Soup
- Chicken and Dumpling Soup
- Carrot Ginger Soup
- Broccoli Cheddar Soup
- Borscht (Beet Soup)
- Ramen Broth (Tonkotsu or Shoyu)
- Wonton Soup
- Duck Confit Soup
- Italian Wedding Soup

- Celeriac Soup
- Zuppa Toscana
- Caldo Gallego
- Beef Consommé
- Japanese Ramen Soup
- White Bean and Kale Soup
- Avocado Soup
- Lobster and Corn Bisque
- Cucumber and Yogurt Soup
- Oysters Rockefeller Soup
- Chilled Cantaloupe Soup
- Fennel and Leek Soup
- Cream of Cauliflower Soup
- Artichoke Soup

Lobster Bisque

Ingredients:

- 2 lobster tails, cooked and chopped
- 4 cups lobster stock (or seafood broth)
- 1/2 cup heavy cream
- 1/4 cup dry white wine
- 1 tablespoon brandy (optional)
- 1/4 cup butter
- 1 small onion, diced
- 2 cloves garlic, minced
- 1/4 cup flour
- 1 teaspoon paprika
- Salt and pepper to taste
- Chopped parsley for garnish

Instructions:

1. In a large pot, melt butter over medium heat. Add onions and garlic, sautéing until soft.
2. Stir in flour and cook for 1-2 minutes.
3. Slowly add lobster stock and white wine, stirring constantly to avoid lumps.
4. Bring to a simmer and cook for 10 minutes, then add the heavy cream and paprika.
5. Add chopped lobster meat and cook for another 5 minutes.
6. Season with salt and pepper, and optionally stir in brandy.
7. Blend the bisque using an immersion blender or regular blender until smooth.
8. Serve hot, garnished with parsley.

French Onion Soup

Ingredients:

- 4 large onions, thinly sliced
- 4 cups beef broth
- 1 cup dry white wine
- 2 tablespoons butter
- 1 tablespoon olive oil
- 1 tablespoon sugar
- 1 tablespoon flour
- 2 cloves garlic, minced
- 1 teaspoon thyme
- 1 bay leaf
- 1 baguette, sliced
- 2 cups Gruyère cheese, shredded

Instructions:

1. In a large pot, melt butter and olive oil over medium heat. Add onions and sugar, and cook, stirring occasionally, until onions are golden brown and caramelized (about 30-40 minutes).
2. Add garlic, thyme, and flour, cooking for 2 minutes.
3. Pour in wine, scraping up any bits from the bottom of the pot. Add beef broth and bay leaf. Bring to a simmer and cook for 20 minutes.
4. Preheat the broiler. Ladle soup into oven-safe bowls, and top each with a slice of baguette and a generous amount of Gruyère cheese.
5. Place bowls under the broiler until the cheese is bubbly and golden brown, about 3-5 minutes.
6. Serve hot.

Cream of Mushroom Soup

Ingredients:

- 2 cups mushrooms, sliced
- 1 small onion, diced
- 2 cloves garlic, minced
- 2 tablespoons butter
- 3 tablespoons flour
- 4 cups vegetable or chicken broth
- 1 cup heavy cream
- Salt and pepper to taste
- Fresh thyme for garnish

Instructions:

1. In a pot, melt butter over medium heat. Add onions and garlic, cooking until soft.
2. Add mushrooms and cook until tender, about 5-7 minutes.
3. Stir in flour and cook for 1-2 minutes.
4. Slowly pour in broth, stirring constantly. Bring to a simmer and cook for 10 minutes.
5. Add heavy cream and cook for an additional 5 minutes.
6. Season with salt and pepper. Use an immersion blender to blend the soup until smooth, or blend in batches.
7. Garnish with fresh thyme and serve.

Roasted Tomato Soup

Ingredients:

- 6-8 ripe tomatoes, halved
- 1 onion, quartered
- 4 cloves garlic, unpeeled
- 2 tablespoons olive oil
- 4 cups vegetable or chicken broth
- 1/2 cup heavy cream
- 1 teaspoon basil
- Salt and pepper to taste
- Fresh basil for garnish

Instructions:

1. Preheat oven to 400°F (200°C). Arrange tomatoes, onion, and garlic on a baking sheet and drizzle with olive oil. Roast for 30-40 minutes, until tender and caramelized.
2. Peel the garlic and transfer all vegetables to a pot. Add broth and basil, bringing to a simmer.
3. Cook for 15-20 minutes, then blend the soup until smooth using an immersion blender or regular blender.
4. Stir in heavy cream and season with salt and pepper.
5. Garnish with fresh basil and serve.

New England Clam Chowder

Ingredients:

- 4 cups clam broth
- 2 cups heavy cream
- 1/2 cup butter
- 1 onion, diced
- 2 celery stalks, diced
- 2 potatoes, peeled and cubed
- 1 teaspoon thyme
- 1 bay leaf
- 2 cups clams, chopped (fresh or canned)
- Salt and pepper to taste
- Fresh parsley for garnish

Instructions:

1. In a large pot, melt butter over medium heat. Add onions, celery, and potatoes, cooking until softened, about 5-7 minutes.
2. Add clam broth, thyme, and bay leaf. Bring to a simmer and cook until potatoes are tender, about 15 minutes.
3. Stir in heavy cream and clams, cooking for an additional 5 minutes.
4. Season with salt and pepper, and remove the bay leaf.
5. Serve hot, garnished with parsley.

Manhattan Clam Chowder

Ingredients:

- 2 tablespoons olive oil
- 1 onion, diced
- 1 bell pepper, diced
- 2 celery stalks, diced
- 2 cloves garlic, minced
- 4 cups clam broth
- 2 cups crushed tomatoes
- 2 teaspoons Worcestershire sauce
- 2 teaspoons hot sauce
- 2 cups clams, chopped (fresh or canned)
- 2 potatoes, peeled and cubed
- Salt and pepper to taste
- Fresh parsley for garnish

Instructions:

1. In a pot, heat olive oil over medium heat. Add onion, bell pepper, celery, and garlic, cooking until softened, about 5-7 minutes.
2. Add clam broth, crushed tomatoes, Worcestershire sauce, and hot sauce. Bring to a simmer.
3. Add potatoes and cook until tender, about 15 minutes.
4. Stir in clams and cook for an additional 5 minutes.
5. Season with salt and pepper.
6. Serve hot, garnished with parsley.

Butternut Squash Soup

Ingredients:

- 1 butternut squash, peeled, seeded, and cubed
- 1 onion, diced
- 2 cloves garlic, minced
- 4 cups vegetable broth
- 1/2 cup coconut milk
- 1 tablespoon olive oil
- 1 teaspoon thyme
- Salt and pepper to taste
- Fresh parsley for garnish

Instructions:

1. In a pot, heat olive oil over medium heat. Add onions and garlic, cooking until soft.
2. Add butternut squash, vegetable broth, and thyme. Bring to a simmer and cook for 15-20 minutes, until the squash is tender.
3. Blend the soup until smooth using an immersion blender or regular blender.
4. Stir in coconut milk and season with salt and pepper.
5. Serve hot, garnished with fresh parsley.

Velouté Soup

Ingredients:

- 4 cups chicken or vegetable broth
- 2 tablespoons butter
- 2 tablespoons flour
- 1/2 cup heavy cream
- Salt and pepper to taste

Instructions:

1. In a pot, melt butter over medium heat. Stir in flour and cook for 1-2 minutes.
2. Gradually add the broth, stirring constantly, until smooth.
3. Bring to a simmer and cook for 10 minutes.
4. Stir in heavy cream and season with salt and pepper.
5. Serve hot.

Chicken Velouté Soup

Ingredients:

- 4 cups chicken broth
- 2 tablespoons butter
- 2 tablespoons flour
- 1/2 cup heavy cream
- 1/2 cup cooked chicken, shredded
- Salt and pepper to taste

Instructions:

1. In a pot, melt butter over medium heat. Stir in flour and cook for 1-2 minutes.
2. Gradually add chicken broth, stirring constantly, until smooth.
3. Bring to a simmer and cook for 10 minutes.
4. Stir in heavy cream and shredded chicken, and season with salt and pepper.
5. Serve hot.

French Pea Soup (Soupe au Pois)

Ingredients:

- 2 cups split peas
- 4 cups vegetable or chicken broth
- 1 onion, diced
- 2 carrots, diced
- 2 cloves garlic, minced
- 1 teaspoon thyme
- 1 bay leaf
- Salt and pepper to taste
- Fresh parsley for garnish

Instructions:

1. In a pot, combine split peas, broth, onion, carrots, garlic, thyme, and bay leaf. Bring to a boil, then simmer for 45-60 minutes, until the peas are tender.
2. Remove the bay leaf and blend the soup until smooth.
3. Season with salt and pepper.
4. Serve hot, garnished with parsley.

Seafood Chowder

Ingredients:

- 4 cups seafood stock
- 1/2 cup heavy cream
- 1/2 cup butter
- 1 onion, diced
- 2 celery stalks, diced
- 1 cup potatoes, peeled and cubed
- 1 cup mixed seafood (shrimp, clams, scallops, etc.)
- Salt and pepper to taste
- Fresh parsley for garnish

Instructions:

1. In a large pot, melt butter over medium heat. Add onions, celery, and potatoes, cooking until soft.
2. Add seafood stock and bring to a simmer. Cook until potatoes are tender, about 15 minutes.
3. Stir in seafood and cook for an additional 5 minutes.
4. Add heavy cream and season with salt and pepper.
5. Serve hot, garnished with parsley.

Crab Bisque

Ingredients:

- 2 cups crab meat (fresh or canned)
- 4 cups seafood or chicken broth
- 1/2 cup heavy cream
- 1/4 cup dry white wine
- 1/4 cup brandy (optional)
- 1/4 cup butter
- 1 onion, finely diced
- 2 cloves garlic, minced
- 1 tablespoon flour
- 1 teaspoon Old Bay seasoning (optional)
- Salt and pepper to taste
- Fresh parsley for garnish

Instructions:

1. In a large pot, melt butter over medium heat. Add onion and garlic, cooking until soft.
2. Stir in flour and cook for 1-2 minutes.
3. Slowly add seafood or chicken broth, stirring constantly to avoid lumps.
4. Add the white wine and bring the mixture to a simmer. Let cook for about 10 minutes.
5. Stir in heavy cream, crab meat, and Old Bay seasoning (if using). Let simmer for an additional 5 minutes.
6. Season with salt and pepper to taste.
7. Blend the soup with an immersion blender or regular blender until smooth (optional).
8. Serve hot, garnished with fresh parsley.

Cream of Asparagus Soup

Ingredients:

- 1 bunch asparagus, trimmed and cut into pieces
- 1 small onion, diced
- 2 cloves garlic, minced
- 4 cups vegetable or chicken broth
- 1/2 cup heavy cream
- 2 tablespoons butter
- Salt and pepper to taste
- Fresh lemon juice (optional)
- Fresh parsley for garnish

Instructions:

1. In a large pot, melt butter over medium heat. Add onion and garlic, cooking until soft.
2. Add asparagus pieces and cook for 5-7 minutes, stirring occasionally.
3. Pour in vegetable or chicken broth and bring the mixture to a simmer. Cook for about 15 minutes, or until the asparagus is tender.
4. Use an immersion blender to puree the soup until smooth or blend in batches.
5. Stir in heavy cream and season with salt, pepper, and lemon juice if desired.
6. Serve hot, garnished with fresh parsley.

Minestrone

Ingredients:

- 1 tablespoon olive oil
- 1 onion, diced
- 2 carrots, diced
- 2 celery stalks, diced
- 3 cloves garlic, minced
- 2 cups diced tomatoes (fresh or canned)
- 4 cups vegetable or chicken broth
- 1 can (15 oz) kidney beans, drained and rinsed
- 1 cup zucchini, diced
- 1 cup pasta (such as elbow macaroni or small shells)
- 1 teaspoon Italian seasoning
- Salt and pepper to taste
- Fresh basil or parsley for garnish
- Grated Parmesan cheese (optional)

Instructions:

1. In a large pot, heat olive oil over medium heat. Add onion, carrots, and celery, cooking until softened (about 5-7 minutes).
2. Add garlic and cook for another minute.
3. Stir in diced tomatoes, broth, beans, zucchini, pasta, and Italian seasoning. Bring to a simmer.
4. Cook for 15-20 minutes, or until the vegetables are tender and the pasta is cooked.
5. Season with salt and pepper to taste.
6. Serve hot, garnished with fresh basil or parsley and grated Parmesan cheese (optional).

Potato Leek Soup

Ingredients:

- 2 tablespoons butter
- 3 leeks, cleaned and sliced
- 2 cloves garlic, minced
- 4 large potatoes, peeled and diced
- 4 cups vegetable or chicken broth
- 1/2 cup heavy cream
- Salt and pepper to taste
- Fresh thyme (optional)

Instructions:

1. In a large pot, melt butter over medium heat. Add leeks and garlic, cooking until softened (about 5-7 minutes).
2. Add diced potatoes and broth, bring to a boil, then reduce to a simmer. Cook for 20-25 minutes, or until the potatoes are tender.
3. Use an immersion blender to puree the soup until smooth, or blend in batches.
4. Stir in heavy cream and season with salt, pepper, and fresh thyme if desired.
5. Serve hot.

Chicken Tortilla Soup

Ingredients:

- 1 tablespoon olive oil
- 1 onion, diced
- 2 cloves garlic, minced
- 1 can (15 oz) diced tomatoes
- 4 cups chicken broth
- 2 cups cooked, shredded chicken
- 1 teaspoon chili powder
- 1 teaspoon cumin
- 1/2 teaspoon paprika
- Salt and pepper to taste
- 1/2 cup corn kernels (fresh or frozen)
- 1/2 cup black beans (optional)
- Tortilla strips (for garnish)
- Fresh cilantro, chopped (for garnish)
- Lime wedges (for serving)

Instructions:

1. In a large pot, heat olive oil over medium heat. Add onion and garlic, cooking until soft.
2. Add diced tomatoes, chicken broth, shredded chicken, chili powder, cumin, paprika, salt, and pepper. Bring to a simmer.
3. Add corn and black beans (if using) and cook for another 10 minutes.
4. Serve hot, garnished with tortilla strips, fresh cilantro, and lime wedges.

Pho (Vietnamese Noodle Soup)

Ingredients:

- 1 lb beef brisket or flank steak
- 1 onion, quartered
- 4 cloves garlic
- 1-inch piece ginger, sliced
- 2 cinnamon sticks
- 2 star anise
- 1 tablespoon coriander seeds
- 1 tablespoon fish sauce
- 4 cups beef broth
- 1 tablespoon soy sauce
- 1 package rice noodles (banh pho)
- Fresh herbs (basil, cilantro, mint)
- Bean sprouts
- Lime wedges
- Sriracha sauce (optional)

Instructions:

1. In a large pot, add brisket, onion, garlic, ginger, cinnamon sticks, star anise, coriander seeds, fish sauce, soy sauce, and beef broth. Bring to a boil, then reduce to a simmer. Cook for 1-2 hours, or until the beef is tender.
2. Remove the beef, strain the broth, and return it to the pot. Slice the beef thinly.
3. Cook the rice noodles according to package instructions, then drain.
4. To serve, place noodles in bowls and ladle the hot broth over them. Top with sliced beef and fresh herbs, bean sprouts, lime wedges, and sriracha sauce.

Miso Soup

Ingredients:

- 4 cups dashi (Japanese fish stock)
- 2 tablespoons miso paste (white or red)
- 1/2 cup tofu, cubed
- 1/4 cup seaweed (wakame, rehydrated)
- 1 tablespoon soy sauce (optional)
- Green onions for garnish

Instructions:

1. In a pot, bring the dashi to a simmer over medium heat.
2. Dissolve the miso paste in a small amount of hot dashi, then stir it back into the pot.
3. Add tofu and seaweed to the soup and simmer for 2-3 minutes.
4. Season with soy sauce if desired and garnish with green onions before serving.

Hot and Sour Soup

Ingredients:

- 4 cups chicken broth
- 1/4 cup soy sauce
- 2 tablespoons rice vinegar
- 1 tablespoon sugar
- 1/2 cup bamboo shoots, sliced
- 1/2 cup mushrooms, sliced
- 1/2 cup tofu, cubed
- 1/4 cup chili paste or sriracha (to taste)
- 1 egg, lightly beaten
- 2 tablespoons cornstarch mixed with 2 tablespoons water
- Green onions for garnish

Instructions:

1. In a large pot, combine chicken broth, soy sauce, rice vinegar, sugar, bamboo shoots, mushrooms, and tofu. Bring to a simmer.
2. Stir in chili paste or sriracha to taste.
3. Mix cornstarch and water to make a slurry, then add it to the soup to thicken.
4. Slowly drizzle in the beaten egg, stirring gently to create ribbons.
5. Garnish with green onions and serve hot.

Tom Yum Soup

Ingredients:

- 4 cups chicken or vegetable broth
- 2 stalks lemongrass, smashed
- 3-4 kaffir lime leaves, torn
- 3-4 Thai bird's eye chilies (or to taste)
- 1 inch piece ginger, sliced
- 1/2 cup mushrooms, sliced
- 1/2 cup shrimp, peeled and deveined
- 2 tablespoons fish sauce
- 1 tablespoon lime juice
- 1 tablespoon sugar
- Fresh cilantro for garnish

Instructions:

1. In a pot, bring the broth to a boil with lemongrass, lime leaves, chilies, and ginger.
2. Add mushrooms and shrimp, cooking until the shrimp turns pink (about 3-5 minutes).
3. Stir in fish sauce, lime juice, and sugar.
4. Serve hot, garnished with fresh cilantro.

Thai Coconut Soup (Tom Kha)

Ingredients:

- 4 cups coconut milk
- 2 cups chicken broth
- 1 stalk lemongrass, smashed
- 3-4 kaffir lime leaves, torn
- 2-3 Thai bird's eye chilies (or to taste)
- 1 inch piece ginger, sliced
- 1/2 cup mushrooms, sliced
- 1/2 cup shrimp or chicken, thinly sliced
- 2 tablespoons fish sauce
- 1 tablespoon lime juice
- Fresh cilantro for garnish

Instructions:

1. In a pot, bring coconut milk and chicken broth to a simmer with lemongrass, lime leaves, chilies, and ginger.
2. Add mushrooms and shrimp (or chicken) and cook until done.
3. Stir in fish sauce and lime juice.
4. Serve hot, garnished with fresh cilantro.

Beef Barley Soup

Ingredients:

- 1 lb beef stew meat, cubed
- 1 tablespoon olive oil
- 1 onion, diced
- 2 carrots, diced
- 2 celery stalks, diced
- 2 cloves garlic, minced
- 6 cups beef broth
- 1/2 cup pearl barley
- 1 teaspoon thyme
- Salt and pepper to taste
- Fresh parsley for garnish

Instructions:

1. Heat olive oil in a large pot over medium heat. Add beef and cook until browned on all sides.
2. Add onion, carrots, celery, and garlic, cooking for 5-7 minutes.
3. Pour in beef broth, pearl barley, thyme, salt, and pepper. Bring to a simmer.
4. Cook for 45 minutes, or until the beef and barley are tender.
5. Serve hot, garnished with fresh parsley.

Gazpacho

Ingredients:

- 6 ripe tomatoes, chopped
- 1 cucumber, peeled and chopped
- 1 red bell pepper, chopped
- 1 small red onion, chopped
- 2 cloves garlic, minced
- 1/4 cup extra virgin olive oil
- 2 tablespoons red wine vinegar
- 1/2 teaspoon cumin
- Salt and pepper to taste
- Fresh basil or parsley for garnish

Instructions:

1. Combine tomatoes, cucumber, red bell pepper, onion, and garlic in a blender or food processor.
2. Blend until smooth, adding olive oil, red wine vinegar, cumin, salt, and pepper. Adjust seasonings as needed.
3. Chill the soup in the refrigerator for at least 2 hours before serving.
4. Serve cold, garnished with fresh basil or parsley.

Cream of Spinach Soup

Ingredients:

- 2 tablespoons butter
- 1 small onion, chopped
- 2 cloves garlic, minced
- 6 cups fresh spinach, washed and chopped
- 2 cups vegetable or chicken broth
- 1/2 cup heavy cream
- Salt and pepper to taste
- Fresh nutmeg (optional)

Instructions:

1. In a large pot, melt butter over medium heat. Add onion and garlic, cooking until softened.
2. Add spinach and cook until wilted, about 5-7 minutes.
3. Add vegetable or chicken broth, bring to a simmer, and cook for another 10 minutes.
4. Use an immersion blender to puree the soup until smooth, or blend in batches.
5. Stir in heavy cream, season with salt, pepper, and a pinch of nutmeg.
6. Serve hot.

Lobster Corn Chowder

Ingredients:

- 2 tablespoons butter
- 1 small onion, diced
- 2 cloves garlic, minced
- 2 cups corn kernels (fresh or frozen)
- 2 cups lobster stock (or chicken stock)
- 1 cup heavy cream
- 1/2 cup cooked lobster meat, chopped
- 1/4 cup white wine (optional)
- Salt and pepper to taste
- Fresh parsley for garnish

Instructions:

1. In a large pot, melt butter over medium heat. Add onion and garlic, cooking until softened.
2. Add corn and cook for 5 minutes, stirring occasionally.
3. Pour in lobster stock (or chicken stock) and white wine, if using. Bring to a simmer and cook for 10 minutes.
4. Stir in heavy cream and lobster meat, cooking for another 5 minutes until heated through.
5. Season with salt and pepper to taste.
6. Serve hot, garnished with fresh parsley.

Split Pea Soup

Ingredients:

- 2 tablespoons olive oil
- 1 onion, diced
- 2 carrots, diced
- 2 celery stalks, diced
- 2 cloves garlic, minced
- 2 cups dried split peas, rinsed
- 6 cups vegetable or chicken broth
- 1 bay leaf
- Salt and pepper to taste
- Fresh parsley for garnish

Instructions:

1. In a large pot, heat olive oil over medium heat. Add onion, carrots, and celery, cooking until softened (about 5 minutes).
2. Add garlic and cook for another minute.
3. Stir in split peas, broth, and bay leaf. Bring to a boil, then reduce to a simmer.
4. Cover and cook for 45-60 minutes, or until the peas are tender.
5. Season with salt and pepper to taste.
6. Serve hot, garnished with fresh parsley.

Pumpkin Soup

Ingredients:

- 2 tablespoons butter
- 1 onion, diced
- 2 cloves garlic, minced
- 4 cups pumpkin puree (or fresh pumpkin, roasted and pureed)
- 4 cups vegetable or chicken broth
- 1/2 cup heavy cream
- 1 teaspoon ground ginger
- 1/2 teaspoon ground cinnamon
- Salt and pepper to taste
- Fresh thyme or parsley for garnish

Instructions:

1. In a large pot, melt butter over medium heat. Add onion and garlic, cooking until softened.
2. Stir in pumpkin puree, broth, ginger, and cinnamon. Bring to a simmer and cook for 15-20 minutes.
3. Stir in heavy cream and season with salt and pepper to taste.
4. Use an immersion blender to puree the soup until smooth.
5. Serve hot, garnished with fresh thyme or parsley.

Sunchoke Soup

Ingredients:

- 2 tablespoons olive oil
- 1 small onion, diced
- 2 cloves garlic, minced
- 1 lb sunchokes (Jerusalem artichokes), peeled and chopped
- 4 cups vegetable or chicken broth
- 1/2 cup heavy cream
- Salt and pepper to taste
- Fresh thyme for garnish

Instructions:

1. In a large pot, heat olive oil over medium heat. Add onion and garlic, cooking until softened.
2. Add sunchokes and cook for 5-7 minutes, stirring occasionally.
3. Pour in broth and bring to a simmer. Cook for 20 minutes, or until the sunchokes are tender.
4. Use an immersion blender to puree the soup until smooth.
5. Stir in heavy cream and season with salt and pepper to taste.
6. Serve hot, garnished with fresh thyme.

Chicken and Dumpling Soup

Ingredients:

- 1 tablespoon olive oil
- 1 onion, diced
- 2 carrots, diced
- 2 celery stalks, diced
- 2 cloves garlic, minced
- 6 cups chicken broth
- 2 cups cooked, shredded chicken
- 1/2 cup frozen peas
- 1 teaspoon dried thyme
- Salt and pepper to taste

For the Dumplings:

- 1 cup all-purpose flour
- 1 teaspoon baking powder
- 1/2 teaspoon salt
- 1/2 teaspoon garlic powder
- 1/2 cup milk
- 2 tablespoons butter, melted
- 1 egg

Instructions:

1. In a large pot, heat olive oil over medium heat. Add onion, carrots, and celery, cooking until softened (about 5 minutes).
2. Add garlic and cook for another minute.
3. Pour in chicken broth, shredded chicken, peas, thyme, salt, and pepper. Bring to a simmer.
4. For the dumplings: In a bowl, mix flour, baking powder, salt, and garlic powder. Stir in milk, butter, and egg, mixing until smooth.
5. Drop spoonfuls of the dumpling batter into the simmering soup.
6. Cover and cook for 15-20 minutes, or until the dumplings are puffed and cooked through.
7. Serve hot.

Carrot Ginger Soup

Ingredients:

- 2 tablespoons olive oil
- 1 onion, diced
- 4 large carrots, peeled and chopped
- 2 inches fresh ginger, peeled and minced
- 4 cups vegetable or chicken broth
- 1/2 cup coconut milk (optional)
- Salt and pepper to taste
- Fresh cilantro for garnish

Instructions:

1. In a large pot, heat olive oil over medium heat. Add onion and cook until softened.
2. Stir in carrots and ginger, cooking for 5-7 minutes.
3. Add broth and bring to a boil. Reduce to a simmer and cook for 15-20 minutes, until the carrots are tender.
4. Use an immersion blender to puree the soup until smooth.
5. Stir in coconut milk (if using) and season with salt and pepper.
6. Serve hot, garnished with fresh cilantro.

Broccoli Cheddar Soup

Ingredients:

- 2 tablespoons butter
- 1 onion, diced
- 2 cloves garlic, minced
- 4 cups broccoli florets
- 4 cups vegetable or chicken broth
- 2 cups shredded sharp cheddar cheese
- 1/2 cup heavy cream
- Salt and pepper to taste

Instructions:

1. In a large pot, melt butter over medium heat. Add onion and garlic, cooking until softened.
2. Stir in broccoli and broth, bringing to a boil. Reduce to a simmer and cook for 15 minutes, or until the broccoli is tender.
3. Use an immersion blender to puree the soup, leaving some chunks if desired.
4. Stir in cheddar cheese and heavy cream, cooking until the cheese has melted.
5. Season with salt and pepper to taste.
6. Serve hot.

Borscht (Beet Soup)

Ingredients:

- 2 tablespoons olive oil
- 1 onion, diced
- 2 cloves garlic, minced
- 4 large beets, peeled and grated
- 4 cups vegetable or chicken broth
- 1/2 teaspoon caraway seeds (optional)
- 1 tablespoon red wine vinegar
- Salt and pepper to taste
- Sour cream and fresh dill for garnish

Instructions:

1. In a large pot, heat olive oil over medium heat. Add onion and garlic, cooking until softened.
2. Stir in grated beets and cook for 5 minutes.
3. Add broth, caraway seeds (if using), and vinegar. Bring to a boil, then reduce to a simmer and cook for 30-40 minutes.
4. Season with salt and pepper.
5. Serve hot, topped with a dollop of sour cream and fresh dill.

Ramen Broth (Tonkotsu or Shoyu)

Tonkotsu Broth Ingredients:

- 4 lbs pork bones (neck or leg)
- 12 cups water
- 1 onion, halved
- 4 cloves garlic
- 2-inch piece of ginger, sliced
- 2 tablespoons soy sauce
- 1 tablespoon miso paste
- 1 tablespoon salt

Shoyu Broth Ingredients:

- 4 cups chicken or pork broth
- 1/4 cup soy sauce
- 1/4 cup mirin
- 1-inch piece ginger, sliced
- 2 cloves garlic, smashed
- 1 tablespoon sesame oil

Instructions:

1. For Tonkotsu broth: In a large pot, bring water, pork bones, onion, garlic, and ginger to a boil. Reduce heat and simmer for 4-6 hours, adding more water as necessary. Strain the broth.
2. Stir in soy sauce, miso paste, and salt.
3. For Shoyu broth: Combine chicken or pork broth, soy sauce, mirin, ginger, garlic, and sesame oil in a pot. Bring to a simmer for 20 minutes, then strain.
4. Serve the broth with ramen noodles and your choice of toppings.

Wonton Soup

Ingredients:

- 1 lb ground pork
- 1/4 cup chopped green onions
- 2 cloves garlic, minced
- 1 tablespoon ginger, minced
- 2 tablespoons soy sauce
- 1 teaspoon sesame oil
- 1/2 teaspoon white pepper
- 1 package wonton wrappers
- 6 cups chicken broth
- 2 tablespoons soy sauce
- 1 tablespoon rice wine
- 2 cups bok choy or spinach, chopped
- Salt to taste

Instructions:

1. In a bowl, combine ground pork, green onions, garlic, ginger, soy sauce, sesame oil, and white pepper.
2. Place a small spoonful of the mixture onto each wonton wrapper. Wet the edges with water and fold into a triangle or a pouch, sealing tightly.
3. Bring chicken broth, soy sauce, and rice wine to a simmer in a large pot.
4. Carefully drop the wontons into the simmering broth and cook for about 5-7 minutes, or until they float.
5. Add bok choy or spinach to the pot, and cook for another 2 minutes.
6. Season with salt to taste.
7. Serve hot.

Duck Confit Soup

Ingredients:

- 2 duck legs, confit
- 4 cups duck or chicken broth
- 1 medium onion, diced
- 2 cloves garlic, minced
- 2 carrots, diced
- 2 celery stalks, diced
- 1/2 cup white wine
- 2 sprigs fresh thyme
- Salt and pepper to taste
- Fresh parsley for garnish

Instructions:

1. Remove the duck meat from the confit and shred it into small pieces. Set aside.
2. In a large pot, sauté onion, garlic, carrots, and celery in a bit of duck fat or olive oil until softened.
3. Add white wine to deglaze the pot, scraping up any bits stuck to the bottom.
4. Pour in the duck broth, add thyme, and bring to a simmer. Let cook for 15-20 minutes.
5. Stir in the shredded duck meat and cook for an additional 5-10 minutes.
6. Season with salt and pepper.
7. Serve hot, garnished with fresh parsley.

Italian Wedding Soup

Ingredients:

- 1 lb ground beef or pork
- 1/4 cup breadcrumbs
- 1 egg
- 1/4 cup grated Parmesan cheese
- 2 teaspoons garlic powder
- Salt and pepper to taste
- 8 cups chicken broth
- 1/2 cup small pasta (like acini di pepe or orzo)
- 2 cups spinach, chopped
- 2 tablespoons olive oil

Instructions:

1. In a bowl, mix ground beef or pork, breadcrumbs, egg, Parmesan cheese, garlic powder, salt, and pepper. Form the mixture into small meatballs.
2. In a large pot, bring chicken broth to a simmer. Gently drop in the meatballs and cook until they float (about 10-15 minutes).
3. Add pasta and cook until tender, about 10 minutes.
4. Stir in chopped spinach and cook until wilted.
5. Drizzle olive oil into the soup for added richness.
6. Serve hot.

Celeriac Soup

Ingredients:

- 1 lb celeriac (celery root), peeled and diced
- 1 large onion, diced
- 2 cloves garlic, minced
- 4 cups vegetable or chicken broth
- 1 cup heavy cream
- 2 tablespoons butter
- Salt and pepper to taste
- Fresh parsley for garnish

Instructions:

1. In a large pot, melt butter over medium heat. Add onion and garlic, cooking until softened.
2. Add celeriac and cook for 5 minutes, stirring occasionally.
3. Pour in broth and bring to a simmer. Cook for 20 minutes, or until the celeriac is tender.
4. Use an immersion blender to puree the soup until smooth.
5. Stir in heavy cream and season with salt and pepper to taste.
6. Serve hot, garnished with fresh parsley.

Zuppa Toscana

Ingredients:

- 1 lb Italian sausage, crumbled
- 1 large onion, diced
- 3 cloves garlic, minced
- 6 cups chicken broth
- 4 large potatoes, thinly sliced
- 2 cups kale, chopped
- 1/2 cup heavy cream
- Salt and pepper to taste

Instructions:

1. In a large pot, cook crumbled sausage over medium heat until browned. Remove and set aside.
2. In the same pot, sauté onion and garlic until softened.
3. Add chicken broth, potatoes, and cooked sausage. Bring to a boil, then reduce to a simmer and cook until the potatoes are tender (about 15 minutes).
4. Stir in kale and cook for an additional 5 minutes.
5. Add heavy cream, and season with salt and pepper.
6. Serve hot.

Caldo Gallego

Ingredients:

- 1 lb smoked pork shoulder or ham hock
- 6 cups chicken broth
- 2 large potatoes, peeled and diced
- 2 cups turnip greens or collard greens, chopped
- 2 cloves garlic, minced
- 1 onion, diced
- 1/2 teaspoon paprika
- Salt and pepper to taste

Instructions:

1. In a large pot, bring chicken broth and smoked pork shoulder or ham hock to a simmer. Cook for about 1 hour until the meat is tender.
2. Remove the pork, shred it, and return the meat to the pot.
3. Add potatoes, garlic, onion, paprika, and cook for another 15-20 minutes, or until the potatoes are tender.
4. Stir in greens and cook until wilted.
5. Season with salt and pepper.
6. Serve hot.

Beef Consommé

Ingredients:

- 2 lbs beef bones (preferably with marrow)
- 10 cups cold water
- 1 onion, quartered
- 2 carrots, peeled and chopped
- 2 celery stalks, chopped
- 1 bouquet garni (parsley, thyme, and bay leaf)
- 2 egg whites (for clarification)
- Salt and pepper to taste

Instructions:

1. Place beef bones in a large pot and cover with cold water. Bring to a boil, then reduce to a simmer. Skim off any scum that rises to the surface.
2. Add onion, carrots, celery, and bouquet garni. Simmer for 4-6 hours, replenishing water as necessary.
3. Remove from heat and strain the broth. Discard solids.
4. To clarify, whisk egg whites into the cooled broth and heat over low heat. Once the egg whites coagulate, strain the broth again through a fine mesh.
5. Season with salt and pepper to taste.
6. Serve hot.

Japanese Ramen Soup

Ingredients:

- 4 cups pork or chicken broth
- 2 tablespoons soy sauce
- 1 tablespoon miso paste
- 2 teaspoons sesame oil
- 1 tablespoon rice vinegar
- 4 ramen noodles (fresh or dried)
- 1/2 cup cooked pork belly or chicken, sliced
- 2 soft-boiled eggs
- 2 green onions, sliced
- Nori sheets (seaweed) for garnish

Instructions:

1. In a pot, combine broth, soy sauce, miso paste, sesame oil, and rice vinegar. Bring to a simmer.
2. Cook ramen noodles according to package instructions and divide into bowls.
3. Pour hot broth over noodles.
4. Top with cooked pork belly or chicken, soft-boiled eggs, green onions, and nori.
5. Serve hot.

White Bean and Kale Soup

Ingredients:

- 1 lb white beans (such as cannellini), soaked overnight
- 1 large onion, diced
- 2 carrots, diced
- 2 celery stalks, diced
- 4 cloves garlic, minced
- 6 cups vegetable or chicken broth
- 4 cups kale, chopped
- 1 teaspoon thyme
- Salt and pepper to taste

Instructions:

1. In a large pot, sauté onion, carrots, celery, and garlic in olive oil until softened.
2. Add soaked white beans and broth. Bring to a boil, then reduce to a simmer and cook for 1-1.5 hours, until the beans are tender.
3. Stir in kale and thyme, cooking for another 10 minutes.
4. Season with salt and pepper.
5. Serve hot.

Avocado Soup

Ingredients:

- 2 ripe avocados, peeled and pitted
- 2 cups chicken or vegetable broth
- 1/2 cup sour cream
- 1 tablespoon lime juice
- 1 small cucumber, peeled and chopped
- 1/4 cup fresh cilantro, chopped
- Salt and pepper to taste

Instructions:

1. In a blender, combine avocados, broth, sour cream, lime juice, cucumber, and cilantro.
2. Blend until smooth and creamy.
3. Season with salt and pepper to taste.
4. Chill the soup in the refrigerator for at least 30 minutes.
5. Serve cold, garnished with additional cilantro if desired.

Lobster and Corn Bisque

Ingredients:

- 1 lb lobster meat, chopped
- 1 ear of corn, kernels removed
- 4 cups seafood stock
- 1 medium onion, diced
- 2 cloves garlic, minced
- 1 medium potato, peeled and diced
- 1/2 cup heavy cream
- 2 tablespoons butter
- 1 tablespoon brandy (optional)
- Salt and pepper to taste
- Fresh parsley for garnish

Instructions:

1. In a large pot, melt butter over medium heat. Add onion and garlic, and cook until softened.
2. Add potato, corn kernels, and seafood stock to the pot. Bring to a simmer and cook until potatoes are tender, about 15-20 minutes.
3. Using an immersion blender, blend the soup until smooth (or leave some texture if preferred).
4. Stir in the lobster meat and brandy (if using), and cook for an additional 3-5 minutes.
5. Add heavy cream and season with salt and pepper.
6. Serve hot, garnished with fresh parsley.

Cucumber and Yogurt Soup

Ingredients:

- 2 large cucumbers, peeled and chopped
- 1 cup Greek yogurt
- 1 tablespoon lemon juice
- 1 tablespoon fresh dill, chopped
- 2 cloves garlic, minced
- 1/4 cup olive oil
- Salt and pepper to taste
- Fresh dill for garnish

Instructions:

1. In a blender, combine cucumbers, Greek yogurt, lemon juice, garlic, olive oil, and fresh dill.
2. Blend until smooth and creamy. If the soup is too thick, add a little water to reach your desired consistency.
3. Season with salt and pepper.
4. Chill the soup in the refrigerator for at least 1 hour before serving.
5. Serve cold, garnished with fresh dill.

Oysters Rockefeller Soup

Ingredients:

- 12 oysters, shucked and chopped
- 2 tablespoons butter
- 1 small onion, diced
- 2 cloves garlic, minced
- 1/2 cup spinach, chopped
- 1/4 cup parsley, chopped
- 1/4 cup breadcrumbs
- 2 cups seafood stock
- 1/2 cup heavy cream
- 1/4 cup white wine
- Salt and pepper to taste
- Lemon wedges for serving

Instructions:

1. In a pan, melt butter over medium heat. Add onion and garlic and cook until softened.
2. Stir in chopped spinach, parsley, and breadcrumbs, and cook for 2-3 minutes.
3. Add the seafood stock and white wine, bringing to a simmer. Let cook for 10 minutes.
4. Add the oysters and heavy cream, and cook for another 5 minutes.
5. Season with salt and pepper.
6. Serve hot, garnished with lemon wedges.

Chilled Cantaloupe Soup

Ingredients:

- 1 ripe cantaloupe, peeled and chopped
- 1/2 cup coconut milk
- 1 tablespoon honey
- 1 tablespoon lime juice
- 1/4 teaspoon ground ginger
- Fresh mint for garnish

Instructions:

1. In a blender, combine cantaloupe, coconut milk, honey, lime juice, and ginger.
2. Blend until smooth and creamy.
3. Chill the soup in the refrigerator for at least 1 hour.
4. Serve cold, garnished with fresh mint.

Fennel and Leek Soup

Ingredients:

- 1 fennel bulb, sliced
- 2 leeks, cleaned and sliced
- 2 tablespoons olive oil
- 4 cups vegetable broth
- 1/2 cup white wine
- 1 medium potato, peeled and diced
- Salt and pepper to taste
- Fresh parsley for garnish

Instructions:

1. In a large pot, heat olive oil over medium heat. Add fennel and leeks, and cook until softened (about 8-10 minutes).
2. Add vegetable broth, white wine, and potatoes. Bring to a boil, then reduce to a simmer and cook for 20 minutes or until the potatoes are tender.
3. Use an immersion blender to puree the soup until smooth.
4. Season with salt and pepper.
5. Serve hot, garnished with fresh parsley.

Cream of Cauliflower Soup

Ingredients:

- 1 medium cauliflower, chopped
- 1 small onion, diced
- 2 cloves garlic, minced
- 4 cups vegetable or chicken broth
- 1/2 cup heavy cream
- 2 tablespoons butter
- Salt and pepper to taste
- Fresh chives for garnish

Instructions:

1. In a large pot, melt butter over medium heat. Add onion and garlic, and cook until softened.
2. Add cauliflower and broth, bring to a simmer, and cook for about 15-20 minutes, or until cauliflower is tender.
3. Use an immersion blender to blend the soup until smooth.
4. Stir in heavy cream, and season with salt and pepper.
5. Serve hot, garnished with fresh chives.

Artichoke Soup

Ingredients:

- 2 cups artichoke hearts, chopped (fresh or canned)
- 1 medium onion, diced
- 2 cloves garlic, minced
- 4 cups vegetable or chicken broth
- 1/2 cup white wine
- 1/2 cup heavy cream
- 2 tablespoons butter
- Salt and pepper to taste
- Fresh thyme for garnish

Instructions:

1. In a large pot, melt butter over medium heat. Add onion and garlic and cook until softened.
2. Add artichoke hearts, white wine, and broth. Bring to a simmer and cook for 15-20 minutes.
3. Use an immersion blender to puree the soup until smooth.
4. Stir in heavy cream, and season with salt and pepper.
5. Serve hot, garnished with fresh thyme.